Red Dirt Dreams

A Collection of Poetry and Prose

Fiona Summerville

Red Dirt Dreams

First Edition

This is a work of fiction. Names, characters, places, and incidents are a product of the author's imagination. Locales and public names are sometimes used for atmospheric purposes. Any resemblance to actual people, living or dead, or to businesses, companies, events, institutions, or locales is completely coincidental.

Copyright © 2019 by Fiona Summerville

All rights reserved. No part of this publication may be reproduced, distributed or transmitted in any form or by any means, without prior written permission.

www.fionasummerville.com

Dedication

To Texas…
and all the wild hearts,
past and present,
that call her home.

Table of Contents

Dedication 3

    Red Dirt Dreams 9
    Seeds of Purpose 10
    Morning Prayer 11
    Moments 13
    Glimmer of Hope 14
    The Road 15
    Fireflies & Fairy Glens 16
    Whiskey Rain 17
    Kindness 18
    Gratitude 19
    Return 20
    Writer's Advice 21
    Chasing Windmills 23
    Daybreak 24
    The Whisper of Peace 25
    Dandelion Hope 27
    Texas Spring 28
    Disciple 29
    Adventure 30
    Paradise 31
    The Spark of Life 33

The Beauty of Grace *35*
Peace in the Pieces *36*
Free for the Taking *37*
Wild Divinity *39*
Chalk Lines *40*
Morning Pages *41*
Last Wishes *42*
Compassion *43*
The Biggest Lie *45*

About the Author **49**

Red Dirt Dreams

May you end each day
with cheeks that ache
from the laughter that refused
to stay buried in your chest.

May the scent of green fields
and sunflowers mix
with the red dirt dreams
that stain your skin

While the madness of Spring
warms your limbs
like those of a new foal finding its stride
in a sun kissed field of flowers
as wild as its soul.

And may you ponder this simple question
as you close your eyes each night
with a vow to do even better
no matter the answer, either way...

"Did you give the world a little more love
than you took from it today?"

Seeds of Purpose

Now we enter the quiet days
the ashen days of dormancy and reflection
when we gather close
to home, hearth and soul fire
and the world draws in upon itself.

From the grandest oak to asphalt weed
soil cradles seed
in a drowsy conspiracy
of the gentle invasion they plan to unleash
upon a world starved of beauty.

So too, do we humans pause,
though not as often as we should,
still somewhere amid all the bustle and rush
of this society designed to strip mine us bare
we find the serenity to plant seeds of purpose
we hope, someday, will blossom into love.

Morning Prayer

I may not kneel
on a man-hewn pew
beneath a steepled roof
at a pre-appointed hour
on a designated day,
but I still pray.

Every moment of everyday
as I bear witness
to the magnificence around me.

The soft crunch
beneath my feet
as I cross the frosty lawn
to catch a better glimpse
of the rose-gold dawn
peeking through
the altar of oak and scrub,

or the soft nicker and snort
of two hungry horses
sharing communion
in a trough
as a chorus of birds
still nestled but stirring
sing Hallelujah
from their branchy lofts,

and let's not forget
the congregation of ducks and geese
paddling their message of peace
across a misty pond.

Why would I trade all this to stand,
my attention transfixed
upon a figure on a cross
raised high above an altar
draped in silks and gold
when the Man being sought
is right here?

Moments

In this camera-ready, digital age
don't worry when you miss the chance
to photograph
the joyful fox scampering through the glade
or the peace of a pink-ribboned sunrise
over the misty lake.

Some moments are meant only
to be captured by your heart.

Glimmer of Hope

Oh, to be filled
once more
with the child-like wonder
that was able to see
swirling dust specks
shimmering
in the late afternoon sun
for what they truly were...

forest sprites and fairies
dusting
a weary world
with a much needed
glimmer of hope.

The Road

Life is a road

that can lead you astray
or lead you home
...get you lost
or get you found

But wherever it leads
always step forward boldly
with an open mind
and heart filled with love
...always love

Fireflies & Fairy Glens

The night was when she came alive.

The night was when her heart took flight.

Soaring over moonbeams
and hop skipping over stars
then floating back to earth
to run free through dew kissed fields
chasing fireflies through fairy glens,
before dawn reclaimed its hold.

Leaving her to daydream
of those fireflies and fairy glens
until they met again once more.

Whiskey Rain

She's like nothing that you've ever seen.
Take you to heaven
on her broken wings
A strike of lightning
followed
by a soothing rain
pouring down
like whiskey burning
until she numbs your pain
She'll love you hard
and leave you wondering
where's she's been all your life
and praying
that she'll choose to stay.

Kindness

There is power in kindness
...in the gentleness of hope

Real power.

In a touch
...a word
...a glance
the knowing silence
of a hug

People won't always see it,
let alone understand it,
so they'll take it for granted
underestimate,
and berate it.

And you'll be hurt
Often.
Time and again
of that I have no doubt
so cry if you must

But don't let the hurt turn bitter.

Don't let the hurt settle in.
If you do, it will change you
...and don't you dare let them change you
because if you do
...they win

Gratitude

Another exhausting day done,
in the quiet of her room
she lay musing
smiling in silent wonder
at the grand manipulation
perpetrated
by her mind and soul
simply so
her eyes may bear witness
to the true magic manifest
within even the most difficult of days
and for that sheer fact alone
she drifted peacefully to sleep,
a sweet whisper of gratitude
lingering
on her softly parted lips

Return

"Return"
the wind whispered
through the maze
of concrete and steel spires.

"Come back"
the woods called
"You've been too long gone
from your home"

And as the crow
flew she followed

Back to the place
verdant reverence
and bare soul
converge

Where her spirit
was free
to chase fireflies
through fairy glens

And hope renewed
became rooted once more

Writer's Advice

As a writer we're told to "write what you know"
and sometimes I do
but more often than not,
I write what I need
...to read...to feel
...to remember...to know

A mantra of sorts, if you will
to keep me moving forward
instead of always looking back.
To help me remember
what the chaos around me
works hard to make me forget.

To focus on hope
(when there is none)
To turn dreams into goals
(when other dreams lay smoldering in the dust)
To love beyond heartbreak
(and again each time, after that)

I refuse to go easy
I refuse to go slow
This journey is mine
and I refuse to let the world tell me
what it is it thinks
I need to know

So I'll write my own advice
and heed it...
at least most of the time
and listen with joy
to the wild ramblings of my heart
and reverently
to the whisperings of my soul

Chasing Windmills

I like chasing windmills
down rust ribbon roads,
cracked by the sun
and lined
by endless fields of dreams
growing wild
on faith
and a splash of sweet southern tea.

Daybreak

The blush of dawn
invades sleepy cerulean
its progress stalled only by
the silent silhouette of geese
landing on still pond

The cool breeze stirs
both leaf and grassy blade
in soft symphony
that accompanies the song
of waking birds

The lone dandelion yawns
stretching wild with pride
to mingle
and entwine itself
with regal rose

As the gentle heart
bearing witness to it all
pours out its blessing
to the budding day
on a sigh.

The Whisper of Peace

The trick, I think,
to cultivating serenity
is to avoid
the garishly mundane
…the blatant places and things
designed to distract and impede
our soul growth,
and to focus instead
on the hushed moments
we so often neglect
in our haste
to *live*.

When was the last time
you paused in awe
of a sunrise
that bleeds
in shades of purpled-pinks
through stubborn clouds of grey

or drove slow enough to notice
the new born foal
tucked deep
in high grass
as it naps
beneath his mother's watchful gaze,

or cast a momentary glance
at the errant roadside patch
of Black-Eyed Susans
so far from the fields
their seeds call home
determined nonetheless
to blossom bright
in a mix
of gravel and harsh red clay.

It's in those precious spaces in time
the whisper of peace is found
inviting us to linger
in its glow
if only for a breath or two.

So why is it,
we seldom do?

Dandelion Hope

Dandelion hope
floats free
on the Springtime breeze
daring even the most barbed wired heart
to dream.

Texas Spring

Step softly as you go
there's wonder brewing
in that unattended place
stirred into being
by the warm breeze of Spring.

Infinite faith revealed
from beneath
the guise of wildflowers
blanketing the earth
in a silent song of praise

Reminding us how
God's grace can transform
even the most barren space
into a garden worthy
of a place in Heaven.

Disciple

Every morning the lavender sky
glows soft in the East
smoldering promise shimmering
from blue grey waves
stoked by the whisper of peace
carried on salted breeze.

And every morning I sit in rapt wonder
as that candy-hued spectacle unfolds
grateful to bear witness,
and maybe,
in some small way,
carry its testament of hope to the world.

Adventure

Dawn broke
the embers of adventure
tinging the long silence
of her wide, wild sky
and so we flew…
blind,
save a tank
brimming with dreams
and the poetry
I read aloud
as you drove.

Paradise

Paradise is what you make it
...a state of mind
...a state of grace

That place inside
that allows you to find peace
along any path you choose,
no matter how it may unspool before you.

That strength you discover
each time you stumble and stop
to pluck bitter thorns
from bruised and calloused feet
as you navigate one blind curve after another
trusting someday the road will smooth and straighten
and all signs along the way will finally point
toward home.

The Spark of Life

Why do we find it so hard to lay our faith in the possibility that there might be something...Someone greater to lean on when we find our endurance waning after running for so long alone no matter the size of the tribe?

Could it be the value we place on the world beyond the infinite Universe we carry within?

Have we become so conditioned by the media hype to want...to desire... to acquire...to adorn ourselves with more than what's truly required for us to feel replete that we're willing to forsake the Spirit within in order to court the fickle purveyors of better, faster, more, and surround ourselves with the noise of those who speak of lighting the darkness while they embrace their night, their gazes fixed on frailty instead of faith, ignoring the true Spark of Life living within their own soul?

I'm old enough now, I think, to admit I've sought out the answers everywhere from the Saturday afternoon confessional, confessing made up sins as a child just to have something to share with a man-appointed conduit between myself and my God, to the incense-hazy metaphysical shops along the winding lost boulevard of dreams, and the ruby-lit space of a tawdry fortune teller's lair.

Yet, somehow, I always knew He was there. Inside me. Even when distraction got the best of me and I veered off course, He waited. Patient, light shining, brimming with grace. He waited for me to realize His was the only light…the only truth I needed. All tucked safely away inside me, until I was ready to receive it.

The Beauty of Grace

Time spares its pace for no one.

Fierce and unyielding
it unspools
a black ribbon
leading to the unknown
leaving
no heart untouched
no soul unturned.

Were it not
for the sweet stillness of grace
we would surely miss
the beauty found in the space
created by
the sharp intake of breath
when transfixed
we bear witness
to a sunset
that ignites
the sleepy marsh
in the soft glow of gratitude
for a waning day
blessed and well spent.

Peace in the Pieces

I've broken more times than I care to admit.
Sometimes as a result of my own foolish follies,
other times, whether willingly or unwittingly,
I found myself woven into the fractured tale
of a soul so bent on their indulgent path
to self-anointed victimhood
they leave a long-suffering debris field of collateral damage
miles wide in their wake.

This pain narrowed my vison.
Sullied the windows of my heart
with a glaze of hopeless dead thought
that left me blinded to the simple wonders of this world
and in a place where I chose
to wallow in the malaise
of the graceless grey landscape
of a disaffected mind and heart
and yet, despite my best efforts to stay,
the light of grace always found me
even in my smallest place
and brought me home.

It's never easy to find peace in the pieces
…or solace at your most sorrow filled time
but in the midst of it all
if you can manage to leave the door open just a crack,
the wild elegance of grace will find you
and sit with you
until you're ready
to find your way back.

Free for the Taking

Life is filled with moments of beauty free for the taking.

Even as we traverse the most desolate of frontiers; when heart and soul fire flicker and fade to what seems like a dying ember and we feel we are doing little more than surviving. When the minutes unfold into hours that unwind into dried husks of unremarkable days we slough off to leave trailing behind, yet at which we forever cast a backward glance to validate our inadequacy and regret at having wasted the precious time we have left.

Even then, there's beauty to be found. But sometimes, no matter how hard we search, the wilderness within has grown to vast and the copse of trees that shields the oasis of our heart has grown too thick and difficult to navigate even though we inherently know the path.

It's those times…when we can't find the beauty within that we need to look out. To seek out the beauty of the world that's been entrusted to us. It's there, in that flash of cardinal red perched upon a barren branch against the backdrop of a grey sky day. Or in the soft nicker and neigh of two spoiled ponies as they wait, patiently impatient for their morning hay. Or in the muffled silence of a snowy landscape, or the gentle cadence of the waves at dawn. Or even in the simple yawn and stretch of a pup who thinks you hang the moon.

The beauty is there, alongside the grace that will give us the strength needed to move forward and through. Both free for the taking. We need only invite them in to that precious unprotected place deep within for them to help light the darkest corners of our heart.

Wild Divinity

Today-

Take that miracle temple your soul calls home out into the wild. And just for a time let your feet of clay become one with the unbridled landscape once more.

Feel the wholeness within you grow from a whisper to a roar as the sacrament of stillness falls feather light upon your heart - wild divinity, fierce and incarnate - after being so long forgotten at the behest of a world terrified by the thought of silence and of the limitless strength solitude with it brings.

Chalk Lines

Reach, plunge deep
beyond bravado and manic mood
straight through
to the spark of hope
that lights the lantern of your soul.

Revel there, bask in its glow
until you're no longer content
to simply step over
the chalk lined silhouettes
that fill this monochrome world.

Choosing instead
to upturn every stone
and fill the fissures
with the agitant palate
of poetry as you go.

Morning Pages

Morning stillness...
thoughts yawn
and stretch out
across the page
slowly
untangling themselves
from sweet nocturnal wanderings
before leaping headlong
into a steaming
hot cup
of sunshine and hope

Last Wishes

When I die,
scatter my ashes
throughout a library
ancient and austere,
so there I may dance
with the dust motes and ghosts
amid the tall winding stacks
of the paper and paste treasures
whose comfort, in life, I revered
alongside a spot of hot honey laced tea
and the sweet purr of love in my lap.

Compassion

May you learn to wield a compassionate hand
with those who navigate this world
with anger as their only compass.
Forever destined
to toil over desolate soil,
with empty hands turned craven claw
eager to scavenge out
seeds of once supple hope
baked dry and turned to husk
after finding no purchase
in endless rows of bitter loam.

The Biggest Lie

"It is what it is," is the biggest lie we tell ourselves. It's a cop out. A pass we give ourselves when either we're too overwhelmed or simply unwilling to make a conscience effort to change. In reality,

IT...this life...this moment... is what we make it, and what we do with whatever we forge soul-fire deep.

Experiences, especially the bad ones, are meant to hone and refine, not to be weaponized.

It's our reaction to each event as it unfolds that is the most telling. It's human nature to take the path of least resistance, and that's easy when we experience a moment of happiness or joy. Those times fall feather light and carry us further down our journey's path.

It's the traumas and tragedies that are the tricky ones to navigate because of the weight they lay heavy upon us. As they bear down, they narrow our vision, shadowing the light we need to see our way clear to move forward. We find ourselves lost along the path we thought we knew. Frozen in place. Too shaken to move on or let go, we give into the fear or anger, no matter how painful, because it's easy. It's there, ripe for the picking and ready to be devoured.

Sometimes we swallow it whole, and let it sink like a bitter brick in the pit of our soul, allowing it weigh us down because it's just easier to wallow, wail and whine about the wrongness of our circumstance than to do the work to shift our thinking in a way that allows us to drag ourselves clear of the quagmire.

But that's where faith and grace come in.

Neither are easy to hold fast to in the dark times, because theirs is not the least resistive path, but those are the times their magic is the strongest. It's that furrowed path littered with time-bombs of self-doubt and resignation that makes us think, search out the truth, no matter how brutal, confront it, then either hone it so that it may be added to our treasure trove of coping skills or let it go. In the process freeing ourselves to grow. If we're willing.

It's the furthest thing from easy, but if you really think about it, things of true value rarely are. They take time, patience and nurturing all of which take focus and oft times excruciating effort, especially in the bleak times. But if we're willing to make the effort we will be rewarded with a strength born of grace.

There's only one difference between love and fear…

Love lasts a lifetime…if you let it.

If you nurture it.

If you do, I promise you, it will flourish and in turn comfort and surround you when the dark days come.

About the Author

Fiona Summerville is a big city, Southern California girl transplanted to a small town in Texas, where she readily indulges her penchant for making things up and scribbling them down.

Before deciding to chase down her dream of being a writer, Fiona made her way through the legal and corporate worlds in stilettos and pencil skirts, as both a Legal and Executive Assistant. Each career was fulfilling in its own unique way, but the call of her muses finally won out, and once she settled in Texas, she began writing in earnest.

In her first two poetry collections, *Only Dark Around the Edges*, and *Typos and All* she dove head first into a myriad of topics with which we all struggle, or find ourselves in the midst of, at one time or another, daring the reader to remember the angst, but never lose sight of the hope and love always waiting on the other side. In her third collection, *Lascivious Intent*, she explored the steamy, and as the title infers, more lascivious side of romance.

In 2017 she left a bit of her heart on the beaches of Kitty Hawk, North Carolina which inspired her fourth collection of poetry, *As Night Falls Hushed*.

Red Dirt Dreams is her shortest, but nonetheless, heartfelt collection inspired by the rugged majesty of her home state of Texas.

When she's not writing, she can be found out with her horses or sipping on a glass of wine while getting lost in a novel or a collection of poetry penned by one of her favorite writers.

You can find her lurking on the following social media sites:

Facebook: facebook.com/FionaSummerville
Twitter: @Fiona_S_Author

Made in the USA
Lexington, KY
18 June 2019